ANIMAL RIGHTS

ANIMAL RIGHTS

Gregory Lee

The Rourke Corporation, Inc.
Vero Beach, Florida 32964

For Pumpkin, Tina Tuna, Louie Louie, and Osa—
they stayed with me for the whole thing.

The Rourke Corporation, Inc.
P.O. Box 3328, Vero Beach, FL 32964

Lee, Gregory, 1956-
    Animal rights / by Lee, Gregory.
        p. cm. — (Troubled society)
    Includes bibliographical references and index.
    Summary: Examines the treatment of animals and explores the issue of whether they have rights.
    ISBN 0-86593-112-7
    1. Animal rights—United States—Juvenile literature. [1. Animal rights. 2. Animals—Treatment.] I. Title. II. Series.
HV4764.L44   1991
179'.3—dc20   91-8565
                                                                   CIP
                                                                   AC
Author's acknowledgements:
Thanks to Jonathan for his timely advice and letting me borrow his one-liners.
My appreciation to Hugh Lofting, too, who had a part in it all.

Series Editor: Gregory Lee
Editors: Elizabeth Sirimarco, Marguerite Aronowitz
Book design and production: The Creative Spark,
    Capistrano Beach, CA
Cover photograph: John Sohm/Chromosohm/The Image Works

Contents

ONE

BLESSED BEASTS?

All animals are equal, but some animals are more equal than others.

—George Orwell, *Animal Farm*

A white rabbit is placed in a small box with a hole just large enough for its neck. Only the rabbit's head is outside the box. The contraption holds the rabbit still while a laboratory researcher puts a substance in the animal's eyes. This is called the *Draize test*, a common lab method to find out if a certain product will cause eye or skin irritation. If it does, the product must carry a warning label before it can be sold to humans. Unfortunately, the rabbit's eyes are permanently damaged in order to find this out.

A cheetah lopes across the African plain, seeking a meal. It stops to observe a herd of zebra grazing in the distance. Suddenly, a rifle shot echoes across the plain, and the cheetah falls. The animal's hide is quickly skinned from its body. Later it will be sold to a furrier who will turn it into part of a jacket or coat for a human to wear. This illegal hunting is called *poaching*.

Four thousand pigs rustle inside a dark, smelly building with a cold, concrete floor. The pigs barely have room to stand up, and they become so uncomfortable that they take to biting at each other's tails. Except they don't have any tails to bite or injure, because the tails were already cut off by humans to prevent any damage to the valuable livestock. Doesn't

This cheetah's fur is a luxury item on the poaching market—which means those who watch over its home in Kenya must be on the lookout for poachers.

it make any difference to the pig ranching industry that cutting off the tail is damage in itself?

A group calling itself the Animal Liberation Front steals 13 beagles from medical researchers at the University of California at Irvine. The beagles were being studied for the physical effects of air pollution, but the liberators said the research was "fraudulent," and so they burglarized the lab and took the animals. Is breaking the law to "rescue" lab animals an act of courage, or an act of criminals?

In this world there are millions of animal species, and humans have still not classified them all. Yet every day more species disappear forever because of the changes in their habitats. Most often, this habitat has been altered by the animal with the most power on earth: the human animal. Because humans have learned to use language and build cities, grow crops and produce electric light, we have become the dominant species on this planet. But our use of the earth's resources, especially animals, is often careless.

Domestication

A few thousand years ago humans learned to train certain animals to live under their control. This is called *domestication*. Goats, chickens, horses and other animals were bred carefully and, in return, the humans made sure the animals were fed and kept safe from predators and harsh weather. When the animals reached a certain age, they were killed for their meat, furs and skins, and any other part of their body that could be used to make tools, clothing or even decorations.

Animals were traded, sold, and herded between groups of people who used them as a way to make their livelihood. Domesticated animals helped make human progress possible by reducing the uncertainty of a food supply. For example, if your only source of food were hunting, you could never be sure there would be food on the table. Bad weather might frustrate the hunt, or disease could kill off your major food source.

Ever since humans realized their power over

animals, they have treated animals as things. Since they were not human, people believed they could not think. They were "inferior." Therefore, animals were here for human use. There was nothing to prevent people from sacrificing animals in religious ceremonies, or hunting them into extinction, or training them for entertainment. Although animals were often idolized in statues, paintings, and even objects of worship, in the end they were almost always killed because it suited the humans who controlled them. Animals had no rights.

The Animal Rights Movement

In the 1990s, this is not quite true anymore. Many humans now talk about animal rights. What is meant by this? Do animals have the same rights to health and happiness as human beings? Do animals have emotions or suffer the way humans do? And if they suffer, do humans have the right or the duty to protect them? What has changed some people's minds about the rights of animals?

A growing number of people in the United States and around the world call themselves animal rights activists. An "activist" is someone who actively participates in promoting and supporting a cause. Their support may take the form of giving money and time to the organization. Activists tell their beliefs to others to gain support. Activists try to persuade their legislators to pass new laws that boost their cause. Occasionally, activists even break laws to get more attention.

Activists in the animal rights movement believe people have harmed and wronged animals

In recent years, apes have been the subject of language studies. These chimpanzees are learning to manipulate a joystick that will produce a simple "language." If we learn to "talk" to the animals, will we still be able to experiment on them?

for too long. They believe animals deserve better treatment. Some disagree about which animals deserve more rights. But this movement has steadily gained support around the world.

We will explore the question of animal rights in this book. People disagree about the best answer. They not only disagree about how animals may be used, but they argue about the basic question: do animals have rights? The answer truly depends on what a person thinks an animal is.

Although the concept of "animal rights" is not new, more people are giving it serious thought than ever before. As we recognize more fully our own fragile existence on this planet, we begin to take the fate of other species more seriously. After all, what has happened to other animals could eventually happen to us.

Darwin

In the 19th century, a naturalist named Charles Darwin did some research that caused a stir in the human world. He concluded that animals and humans shared the same biology. That is, he said all creatures, including humans, were descended from the same beginnings of life on earth. For instance, apes and humans share many physical characteristics. By studying our genes, scientists can tell that apes and humans have a common biological heritage. We are both part of the animal family called *primates*.

When people started to learn enough about the similarities between animals and humans (instead of just our obvious differences), some began to wonder whether we should treat animals any differently than humans. For example, humans think it is wrong to hunt one another for food. Humans do not dissect other humans alive in laboratories to study the insides of their bodies. Humans do not cage humans so that other humans can look at them. Why is it okay to treat animals in such ways, but not other people?

Those who believe humans are superior to other species on earth say we are justified in using animals as we please. The use of animals for medical research, for example, has produced new vaccines and surgical methods that have saved countless human lives. Isn't that alone worth it?

It is easy to criticize the destruction of an animal for its fur and make us feel pity for that animal. It is difficult to ignore, however, the ritual of life on this planet as it has been lived for millions of years. Hunting has been a natural part of humankind's life since the beginning of history. Humans are omnivorous mammals, meaning we eat both plants and meat—other animals—to survive.

Most of the animals that animal rights activists want to protect are meat eaters, too. Cats and dogs, of course, eat meat. Left alone, these animals could catch and eat their prey just like wild animals do. Should humans feel guilt or concern over their own biological heritage?

Double Standards

Even people who support animal rights sometimes have a "double standard"—one rule for humans and one rule for other species. Some people think it is cruel to use dogs and cats in medical research, but do not feel the same way about rats and mice. After all, rats and mice are smaller, may carry disease, are not as intelligent as household pets, and don't give affection—at least in ways that humans prefer. They aren't so cute and cuddly.

We can go even further. Some people who would never eat meat may not think twice about killing a spider or a cockroach in their house. Insects get no respect in our society, and we kill them easily by the millions every day with insecticide sprays, "roach motels," and even rolled-up magazines. We smash, spray and stomp insects with relief. Why? Because they're "pests," "bugs," and "filthy."

Notice the change in vocabulary: pets are cute, but insects are bugs. They bug us. Since they're not pleasant and fun, it's all right to squish them.

Speciesism

Some of the animal rights groups with the strongest views believe talking about animals in different terms is like racism. Animal rights philosopher Peter Singer calls this *speciesism*—treating certain species as lesser forms of life. In our society, there are rules for "us," and rules for "them." Keeping animals ("them") separate, in the way we talk and act, makes it easier for us humans to treat them differently. Racism is like that, and animal rights advocates say that speciesism is a similar problem.

The speciesism argument asks: If our intelligence prevents us from using other humans for our own selfish purposes, why do we exclude beings that are not of our species?

Is it immoral to treat animals differently? For

thousands of years, humankind has tamed animals for its own use. We make clothes from animal skins and eat animal flesh for food. Not all animals we raise, however, are killed for meat. Indirectly, captive animals or livestock are used for their by-products. For example, cows provide milk which is turned into dairy products such as yogurt and cheese. Sheep provide wool. These animals eat, sleep, and breed under strict conditions supervised by humans to maintain quality. Is this cruel, or would such animals be any better off as "wild" life?

The domestication of animals is considered a turning point in human civilization. By domesticating animals, we entered into a relationship that is beneficial to both the human and animal: we feed the animal and protect it, and in return the animal gives us wool or milk or fur. Of course, this sometimes means sacrificing the animal, but not until after it has led a useful adult life (measured by our human standards, that is).

Historians believe the domestication of animals helped the human species develop modern, technological societies more quickly. As our ability to raise and grow food became more efficient, less time was spent in the gathering of food. More time could be devoted to developing our minds, and our culture was born. Some say we built our lives of relative comfort on the backs of the rest of the earth's species. But our treatment of animals can range from extreme pampering to horrible abuse.

Humane Versus Inhumane

When an animal shelter in New York was found

How Do Americans Feel About Animal Rights?

Here are some results from a 1990 opinion poll that indicates some of what Americans feel about animal rights.

• 80 percent agreed that animals have rights that should limit how humans use them.

• 63 percent said that killing animals to make fur coats should be illegal. Another 22 percent didn't believe in killing animals for fur, but didn't think it should be against the law.

• 69 percent are against killing animals for leather.

• 60 percent disapprove of hunting for sport, but 85 percent said it's okay to kill animals for food.

• A majority of people also believe that zoos, animal shows, and using animals in medical research is acceptable (78 percent said they were in favor of using animals for AIDS research).

• 60 percent said that humans should avoid actions that would cause a species to become extinct, like building a dam over a rare habitat. But 30 percent said it would depend on the specific case.

to have 400 animals crammed into one-quarter of an acre, the County of Westchester cited the owner for cruelty to animals. County officials threatened to close the facility because it was unhealthy—not for humans, but for animals. The owner had refused to put the unwanted animals to death, which led to filthy, crowded conditions. So which is more humane: death or prolonged discomfort?

Laws in many countries have recognized for a long time that animals deserve decent treatment, food and shelter. In fact, concern for animals and their treatment is not new at all. Many people were concerned about how animals were treated centuries ago. But there has always been a double standard, or two ways of looking at the meaning of "humane," especially when it came to animals we like to eat.

Pets

If people want to consider what they can do about animal rights, they should try looking in their own back yard. People who let their household cats wander around outdoors, for instance, think their pets can defend themselves. "Cats are independent," is a phrase we often hear. But disease, hunger, and automobiles kill many pets every year. Domestication means that humans bear responsibility for the welfare of the animals they own. But this responsibility is not always taken seriously.

Consider the common practice of declawing the family cat. Cats have sharp claws for defense. People declaw their cats because they often ruin furniture or shred wallpaper with frequent scratching.

But many owners who declaw their cats also let them roam freely around the neighborhood, which means their animals are now defenseless, and can be seriously hurt by other cats or dogs.

Veterinarians can tell horror stories of pets brought in for emergency care by owners who said the animals had "fallen" or were hit "accidentally." Unfortunately, many of these pets had been physically abused deliberately. Broken jaws, broken limbs, loose teeth and other injuries are not uncommon.

Many people breed dogs and cats for profit. Certain breeds are exotic, rare, and very expensive. Purebreds are a big business. As a result, in the United States alone, more than one million dogs were bred in 1989. The demand, unfortunately, is not great enough to find homes for all those dogs. And these are just the registered purebreds. This doesn't count the millions of litters that are born to stray cats and dogs each year (or in family homes, where people have trouble just giving them away). Many animals are abandoned on country roads and city streets. Abandoned animals face short, unhealthy lives in the "wild" of America's cities and towns. While Americans spend $8 billion on pet products each year, millions of potential pets—cats and dogs from unwanted litters—die. Local humane societies try to help save many unwanted animals, but there are never enough homes for all of them. As a result, city and county animal shelters have to practice *euthanasia* (putting the animals to death).

So the question remains: do animals have some rights? no rights? any rights? If they have some rights, when will humans recognize them?

TWO

THE RESEARCH CONTROVERSY

Perhaps the one area where animal rights activists and "humans first" activists disagree most is in the area of using animals for medical research. Each year rats, mice, dogs, cats, and primates are subjected to medical research tests in laboratories.

Sometimes the animals are exposed to chemicals or products to see if they are harmful. Some animals receive treatment or surgery to learn if a new medical technique will work properly. After much testing (in some studies, many years later), the laboratories can usually report if the process is safe for humans. In the case of drugs, the federal Food and Drug Administration (FDA) must okay all drugs before they can be prescribed for human use.

Animal rights activists feel this medical research testing is not fair to animals. Why should other species sacrifice their lives in order to advance medical science for humans? Some people believe we have the right because we are human, because no other animal on earth can shape its environment like humans. And no other animal has the knowledge or skills to create new things like humans do. We appear to be masters of the earth.

Religions have also reinforced the idea of human superiority over animals. A famous French philosopher named Descartes said that animals were "soulless machines." This has been a typical human attitude for centuries.

But if we are sensitive enough to question our right to dominate other species—or at least feel some

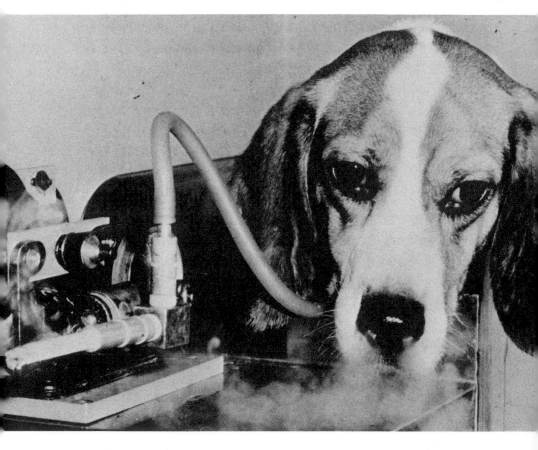

A beagle becomes a chain smoker in this New Jersey medical lab. The dog "smokes" through a machine linked to its windpipe by a tube. This experiment was designed to study the connection between smoking and the lung disease *emphysema*.

guilt—then are we certain of our right to use animals as we please? Apparently not all human beings are satisfied with our superior stand, and so the animal rights debate has grown.

The Numbers

The U.S. Department of Agriculture (USDA) reported that 1,635,288 animals were used in testing and research in 1988. Incredibly, this total does not include rats, mice, birds, and livestock. If we include these animals, the figures are huge. The U.S. Office of Technology Assessment (OTA) stated that in 1983 (the last year figures were compiled), between 17 and 22 million animals were actually used in biomedical and product research.

Do these seem like high numbers? Is it necessary to confine, infect, operate on and eventually kill this many animals every year? The National Academy of Sciences claims the numbers have actually declined, down from 38 million in 1968!

What Is Medical Research?

Hundreds of years ago humans started to learn more about anatomy and illness by studying dead human bodies (called *cadavers*) and living animals. Cutting open a live animal to study it is called *vivisection*. Humans learned a lot about health and why we get ill by studying animal anatomy. People studying to be doctors have had to work on both living animals and cadavers to learn their job. You can't know how to repair a wound, or remove a diseased organ, unless you've practiced on real tissue.

Even though today's technology allows doctors to examine, diagnose, and even cure many illnesses without surgery, no one can become a doctor without actual experience with human and animal tissue in medical school. The same surgical procedures have to be performed by students over and over again, year after year.

Supporters of animal research cite more than 40 Nobel Prize-winning scientists whose work often depended on using animals. Some vaccines developed through animal experimentation prevent polio, diphtheria, mumps, measles, rubella and smallpox.

LD-50

To animal rights activists, one of the most objectionable things done in research is the so-called LD-50 test. LD stands for "lethal dose." In an LD-50 test, the object is to find out how much of a substance will kill half the animals in a test group. For example, how much shoe polish will 100 rats have to eat (or be forced to eat) before at least 50 of them die? The quantity that is harmful enough to be lethal is called the toxicity level. Many LD-50 tests are conducted by injecting the substance directly into an animal, since it is not always possible to force it into the animal any other way.

Because of repeated protests, there has been a big decline in the use of the LD-50 test. The FDA says the number of LD-50 studies has declined 96 percent since the 1970s because alternative methods of testing have been found. Some use special bacteria (called a *culture*), while others use computer models.

When using a cell culture, researchers want to see if the culture will mutate (change). This can be a quick indication of whether a substance can cause cancer or other problems. However, most researchers insist this is a good way to screen many chemicals, but not to judge which ones should be tested further on live subjects.

The lethal dose test is not the only one where

animals are exposed to possibly harmful substances. Researchers also test the effectiveness of new drugs and check for unwanted side effects. For some research, experts believe that no substitute exists for using a live subject, as the interaction within a living body is what needs to be judged. Simply put, what is good for your liver may not be good for your stomach. It is therefore necessary to watch a new drug travel through an entire living body, and then the results must be compared with similar tests to make sure the effect is the same.

Do Animals Suffer?

Perhaps the greatest concern to those who protest animal research is that we know animals feel pain. Although there is still some debate about how human pain may differ from other species, it is clear that pain is common to all animals with nervous systems. This is obvious, especially in mammals, because they will make attempts to flee or stop a source of pain. They make noises that signal discomfort. If you have ever accidently stepped on your cat's tail, you know what this sounds like.

A USDA study in 1985 reported that only six percent of animals used in research were allowed to feel pain (because it was part of the experiment). This study, once again, did not include rats or mice, the animals most commonly used in all forms of lab research. Is six percent okay? Or is any percent wrong?

Animal rights activists say that human beings would not permit the same experiments on other humans. For example, a person named Fred is mentally retarded, meaning he has no ability to do many simple things that most of us would call "normal." Fred can't care for himself, and he understands little of what he sees or hears. He can't do anything difficult like work at a regular job or go to school. In fact, Fred will never be able to function as well as a ten-year-old "normal" child. By some people's standards, he is no more aware and alive than many animals. So would it be all right to experiment on Fred? Since he is a human being, his reactions to chemicals, radiation, new foods, and treatments would be similar to those of other humans. A study of his nervous system, vital organs, and brain would be more revealing than the same study of a horse or a mouse. Wouldn't this make sense?

Of course not. No one would allow such testing. Everyone would say the idea was barbaric—plain wrong. So why is it okay to treat animals this way? This is the moral dilemma that animal rights activists are concerned about.

On the other hand, those who support the use of animals in research say that animals are different than humans. Because humans can think, solve problems, and change their environment more than any other species on earth, that gives them the right to use other animals. After all, if we are the masters, we should be able to benefit from our own intelligence. Many people also feel the benefits of animal research far outweigh emotional concerns. If a drug will save human lives—but only after it is tested on animals—most people will not hesitate to say that the animals should be sacrificed.

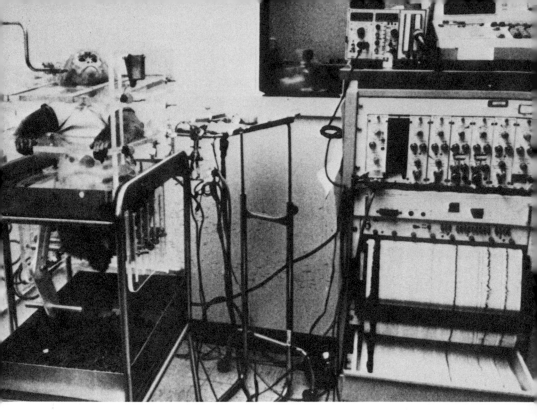

In this research lab, a pregnant rhesus monkey is having her blood monitored around the clock. She must be restrained in a chair to accomplish this.

Should Science Be Restricted?

Many scientists do not like too much government regulation regarding their research. They fear that banning certain types of research will limit their freedom and independence. Americans are highly suspicious of such restrictions. In Europe during the Middle Ages, early scientific work was permitted only when it did not contradict the state's religion. But in the United States today, most poeple don't believe that governments or special interest groups should control the search for knowledge.

Science has become so important in our society that research is often sheltered. In other words, laboratories are kept private, and few people know what really happens in many experiments. But are science and scientists perfect? Should their work be kept secret from the public? Recent events have lessened the trust some people have in science. For example, the explosion at the Chernobyl nuclear power plant in the Soviet Union, and the explosion of the space shuttle *Challenger* made people wonder how such accidents could have happened. And the atomic bomb is one of the most frightful examples of science that was used—not for knowledge—but for power. This single invention has cast a shadow over the world for nearly half a century.

The area of medical knowledge that has benefited most from using animal vivisection is in the treatment of heart and circulatory problems. Heart surgery, heart transplants, and other operations on human veins and arteries were first tested on animals—particularly dogs. Repairing damaged blood vessels, heart valves, and other tissues has been achieved after much study and practice on animals. Since cardiopulmonary disease is the biggest killer every year in America, surgeons are convinced that research on other species has saved countless human lives.

Other benefits from vivisection are harder to demonstrate. Would a new vaccine have still been developed without experimentation? If animal experiments had not been used, would a new way to achieve the same results have been found? These are hypothetical questions, however, because they cannot be answered based on real events or statistics. No one will ever know.

As mentioned earlier, researchers fear that

putting too many restrictions on animal research will limit their ability to discover new medicines, new surgical procedures, and new cures. They also say that many animal rights advocates do not understand or are poorly informed about the laboratory treatment of animals. For example, the Animal Welfare Act of 1966 requires specific standards for animal treatment. These standards are listed in a government book called the *Guide for the Care and Use of Laboratory Animals.* But there is much dispute over whether these standards are followed often enough, and it is difficult for the government to monitor and inspect every animal testing laboratory.

Cosmetic Testing

The cosmetics industry makes lipstick, perfume, eye makeup, deodorants, and other products that Americans use every day. Whether for beauty or hygiene, we spend billions of dollars every year to look pretty and smell good. But did you know that the federal government requires every new cosmetic to be tested first to make sure it won't harm consumers?

Cosmetics companies used to test their products on animals, but in the past few years many have stopped this practice. They found it was better to advertise products that are "cruelty free"—not tested on animals. The People for the Ethical Treatment of Animals (PETA) claims it has forced some 200 cosmetics companies to stop animal testing.

There is, in fact, no law that requires a company to test the safety of a product on animals. The FDA only requires that a firm be able to demonstrate product safety. Until recently, the use of animals has merely been the most convenient method. The FDA relies heavily on the results of animal testing, which is probably why it remained so popular for so long.

One test still used in cosmetics testing is the Draize test, as mentioned in Chapter 1. This is where an animal, usually a rabbit, is exposed to a substance placed on its eye. Since rabbit eyes have no eyelid or ability to form tears, the animal cannot clean out its eye, and it will show the effects of the substance. The effects of that substance on human eyes can be predicted because of the rabbit's reaction, but the animal's eyes are damaged in the process.

Under pressure from animal rights groups, many cosmetics companies have stopped using the Draize test. It is hard to justify harming animals to test substances which are not really vital to human life. Most people are likely to agree that lipstick and cancer research are not of equal importance to the welfare of men and women.

Behavioral Testing

For the past 100 years, humans have used animals to test many theories about behavior. The study of behavior is called *psychology*. For example, by testing an animal's reaction to a controlled event (like the reward of food), a psychologist will propose a theory that predicts human behavior. Behavioral studies are often designed to measure an animal's ability to learn or memorize something. This implies that by studying animal intelligence more may be learned about human intelligence.

Some behavioral studies have come under fire, however, for treating animals cruelly. Baby

Animal Lab Controversy

Some animal experiments have been so violent and caused such misery that they have been stopped by protest. One incident that raised a great outcry in 1984 involved the University of Pennsylvania's Experimental Head Injury Laboratory. Videotapes of experiments done there were stolen by animal rights advocates and made public. The videotapes showed baboons being struck on the head by metal pistons until their skulls were broken. Other primates were shown being operated on without pain killers.

The reason for the study? Researchers wanted to classify the most common types of head injuries (like those that might occur in a car accident) so they could be easily recognized. Learning to recognize the cause of an injury by examining its after-effects can help law enforcement solve a crime, for instance.

The suffering of hundreds of baboons used in the University's experiments, however, was too much even for most pro-research people to bear. The revelations ended this research, and the U.S. Office of Technology Assessment recommended that in the future, Congress ban certain animal uses and cut off funding to anyone violating the bans.

chimps have been deprived of their mothers by being placed in special cages where they received no reassuring stimulation. They are given no light, no warmth, no fur to hold, and little food. These kinds of experiments have been repeated in labs across America for years, and the results are always the same: a lot of depressed chimps (or monkeys or baboons) with little will to live. Studies like this are done repeatedly because researchers don't want to rely on another researcher's results. They want to use their own findings to prove a theory and publish the results.

This is the form of animal testing that has received the harshest criticism. Besides the obvious cruelty involved, the usefulness of the results is questionable. Researchers will say they must use animals to help understand human behavior, but to avoid criticism that they are harming sensitive species, they go out of their way to talk about their "subjects" in ways that are unemotional. In research papers, for example, they avoid using human, emotional terms to describe the animals' reactions. The question is, if the test animals are so unlike human beings, then how can the results predict anything about human behavior?

The 1990s are likely to see a severe reduction in animal behavior tests. This is because many of these experiments are the projects of college students who are trying to repeat results already made public. And since many people oppose these tests, why repeat them again with more animals—especially when there is no doubt that the results will be the same?

THREE

HUNTING AND WILDLIFE

Hunting is the one area where the animal welfare activists may have the least effect in changing public policy. The right to hunt in America is closely tied to the right to bear arms, which is guaranteed by the Second Amendment of the Constitution. People who oppose hunting are accused of really wanting to take guns away from people, which any hunter will tell you is a constitutional right. States can and do limit the purchase, sale, type, and legal uses for guns, but they are forbidden by the Constitution to do away with the right to own a gun entirely. And many people own a gun because they enjoy hunting.

Hunting is also an environmental issue, with some animal populations threatened when their numbers grow too large. The U.S. Bureau of Land Management (BLM) has authorized "kills" of wild species when they threaten to destroy the habitat of another. But hunts are supposed to be strictly controlled, and hunting seasons are limited to a few weeks or months duration. Just because some hunting is prohibited by law, however, does not mean that all animals are protected or that no one hunts out of season. Some people ignore these laws.

In other countries, too, certain animals are protected because they are endangered. For example, elephants have long been off-limits to hunters in Asia and Africa. The large numbers hunted in the past century (mainly for the ivory in their tusks) threatened them with extinction. But laws against

For two centuries hunters have killed elephants for their ivory tusks. This herd in the African country of Namibia lives in a national park, where the authorities try to protect them from poachers.

hunting (called poaching) are hard to enforce. Poachers kill and then leave most of their prey behind (often creating orphans at the same time). Some countries try to discourage poaching by banning the importation of products known to be made from materials like ivory. But then humans will resort to smuggling, breaking even more laws. This raises the price of the scarce material, which means poaching becomes more profitable. And so more illegal killing occurs.

The morality of hunting is an even stickier issue for people to agree on, like discussing one's religion. People who enjoy hunting will talk about how nature makes animals hunters so that they can survive. Animals eat other animals and—so this argument goes—humans were made to do the same. Responsible hunters never kill more than they can reasonably eat, and they say they are helping nature control animal overpopulation. It is an argument borrowed from the work of Darwin, the scientist who claimed humans and animals share common ancestors.

Hunters, of course, also enjoy the thrill of the kill. They say it is a powerful human urge, and stalking an animal is exciting. Hunting has been made into a "sport" by hunting clubs, hunting preserves (parks), and hunting magazines. Some people believe this desire to kill another animal merely for "sport" is wrong. But hunters say they are not being cruel, that the animals they hunt die swiftly, and that they never hunt beyond the legal limits. Whether humans should have the right to hunt other species, however, is an issue that has no scientific answer.

Fishing

Millions of Americans love to fish. Fishing, like hunting, is regulated by states to prevent the stock of fish in lakes and streams from disappearing completely. Most people enjoy eating fish, and many have no trouble killing and cleaning their own fish for a meal.

Fish are a lot less cuddly than a dog or a cat. Their nervous systems are not as sophisticated as mammals. So we place fish farther down the order of animal species, which makes it easier for us to treat them more like things than living beings. Still, when a fish is caught, it is brought into the fishing boat where it flops around until it dies. The fish suffocates because it needs water to breathe.

Does a fish feel any pain? We probably can never know for sure. Even some people who believe in animal rights are not too interested in extending rights to fish, shrimp and oysters. It is up to individuals to decide if it matters.

Tuna And Dolphins

There is one fishing practice, however, that has come under fire from animal rights groups: the way tuna are caught at sea. Tuna boats use huge nets that drag the ocean bottom in order to catch the greatest number of fish in one haul. These nets are dragged on board the fishing boat and then emptied.

Tuna swim in schools, so when fishermen use this method, they catch thousands of fish at one time. But other animals are often caught with the tuna. Dolphins in particular are often tangled in tuna nets, where they suffocate underwater because they need to surface to breathe. Before the nets are hauled out, many dolphins have literally drowned.

In April 1990 three American food companies announced they would no longer buy tuna that had been caught in nets that harm dolphins. These three companies (H.J. Heinz Co., Van Camp Seafood Co., and Bumble Bee Seafoods Inc.) sell more than 70

Many species of whale have been hunted to near extinction.

percent of the canned tuna in the United States. They were pressured by protest groups that wanted to stop the use of the huge nets responsible for killing up to 100,000 dolphins each year. With this ban the change has started to save dolphin lives.

Whaling

Another ocean controversy is whale hunting. Some species of whales were nearly hunted to extinction in the last 100 years. Because of their size, whales produce great quantities of oil, meat, and blubber that are converted into many products. The hunting of whales was very efficient. Large harpoons were used to spear the animals. Modern harpoons are even more efficient. They feature explosive heads that burst inside the animal, killing them quicker.

As the whales began to disappear, however, nations became concerned about losing these beautiful animals forever. Even nations that depended heavily on whaling for trade were concerned, fearing their business might die off forever. So the International Whaling Commission (IWC) was formed, and this body meets regularly to control whaling in the oceans. All nations that have regular whaling industries participate.

The IWC became so concerned about certain species that they declared a moratorium on hunting them. No nation could hunt these species at all until the ban was lifted. And yet some countries have been found violating these bans repeatedly. The worst violators are Norway, Japan, and the Soviet Union. The IWC is like the United Nations: it can declare something wrong, but it has very little power to enforce its laws.

People have taken a greater interest in whales because research has found that whales have high intelligence. They emit audible squeaks, wails, and growls that are called "songs," and these songs can be heard underwater by other whales from great distances. This communication, even though humans can't understand it, has regular patterns, and seems to convey information that only whales understand. Since discovering that whales have this capability, many people believe all hunting of whales should end forever.

People who oppose the raising of animals for expensive fur coats demonstrate outside a Beverly Hills store.

Hunting For Fur

Many fur-bearing animals such as chinchilla and mink are now raised on farms. Others, however, must still be caught in the wild. Trapping is an ancient hunting method, where people often use devices that grab an animal's leg when an animal steps on it. Modern steel traps have "jaws" that can crush an animal's bone. An unlucky animal may remain in a trap for days before the trapper returns to check it. The animal will usually die of starvation or shock before the trapper can arrive to kill it. Some animals gnaw their own limb off to escape. So brutal is this form of hunting that more than 60 countries now ban the leg-hold trap. The United States does not.

For several years the group Greenpeace has protested the hunting of baby harp seals along the northeastern shore of Canada for their fur. It is almost traditional that groups of humans cluster around the small, white animals and club them to death. Fur from these creatures is banned in the United States.

FOUR

Raising Food

The United States is often called the "bread-basket of the world."

That expression means we produce more food for more tables than any other nation on earth. Our natural resources are abundant. Our economic wealth and modern farming methods are also important factors. And our skill in raising animals for food is unmatched.

Animals raised for food are called livestock. When animals were first domesticated, livestock became a primary way that humans lived and survived on earth. Today, raising livestock has become highly specialized. Breeding and feeding techniques are highly controlled and follow years of scientific testing and experimentation. What does this mean to the livestock?

Many of these animals spend their entire lives penned in cramped cages and fed special diets until they reach a certain age. Then they are killed for our dinner table. We raise certain animals for their flesh, then we eat them. We call this agriculture. Animals in the wild don't go through the steps we humans do to get their dinner, but the result is the same. They catch their prey, kill it, and then eat it. It is a natural way of life that is as old as the earth itself.

The Factory Farm

We used to talk about the "family farm." Now it is more accurately called the "factory farm." Animals in the United States are mass produced at a staggering rate. On farms today, a species' natural

Hundreds of chicks begin their new lives in this Maryland chicken coop. They will be raised as broilers—the kind of chickens packaged in your local grocery store.

environment is modified to produce the most food out of each animal. This may be just good business, but it can also mean that animals being fattened for our dinner table are treated inhumanely.

Try to imagine six egg-laying hens confined in a 12- by 20-inch cage. There is no room for them to do natural things like cleaning their own feathers. The wire walls of the cage rub much of their feathers from their bodies. Chickens are literally on top of other chickens for a year or more. Imagine living in a bunk bed with four of your friends for a year and you might understand a hen's frustrating life.

At least hens live a little longer than male chicks. Egg farming and raising chickens for meat are generally two separate businesses. Since egg farmers have no use for male chicks, they are destroyed right after they hatch. Sometimes they are gassed, or tossed into trash bags atop their fellow chicks to suffocate. It's estimated that every year at least 160 million birds die this way.

You might think that chickens raised for their meat have an easier life: they stand around all day and eat, then their life is ended. Right? Wrong. Eating chickens aren't left untouched during their short lives. For one thing, they have to be "debeaked." Because the birds are raised in over-crowded buildings and are under stress, they soon begin to peck and even eat each other. This is bad for business, because pecked poultry is unsalable. So a special cutting device was invented that ampu-tates the birds' beaks while they are young. This is almost like having your nose cut off—without any pain killer.

A pig's life is no better. Thousands are crammed into giant buildings where there is barely room enough to lie down. They are kept in the dark for weeks, where they walk in their own *excrement* (body waste). This causes foot infections. The smell is horrible, but the polluted air is worse on their lungs.

The overcrowding produces behavior prob-lems in pigs as it does with chickens. But instead of giving the pigs more room, the building is kept dark to help keep stress down. And the pigs usually have their tails cut off too.

Cattle are fattened with special diets and given drugs so they will have the most meat possible when they are slaughtered. Their lives consist of eating, eating, and eating. When they get big enough, they are jam-packed into trucks or railroad cars and taken on long journeys with few stops for food and water.

At the slaughterhouse they are stunned with an electric shock, have their throats cut, and then hung upside down so the blood drains out. Butchering has never been clean or easy, but with today's methods cattle can be slaughtered at a rate of 275 animals per hour.

Some baby beef are used to produce a product called veal. A restaurant menu listing veal is boasting of fine dining. But these calves spend their entire lives isolated in separate pens that are only one-foot, ten-inches wide by four-feet, six-inches long. They do not eat, drink, suckle, defecate or urinate in any other place but this same pen. A slanted floor allows their waste matter to be washed away. This is their entire existence. A mortality rate between 10 and 15 percent is not unusual on veal ranches.

Why are these animals allowed so little freedom of movement? In the case of cattle and pigs, the answer is simple: the more the livestock move around, the more weight they will burn off. And less weight means less meat, which means less money when the livestock is sold. With veal calves, restricting their movements also keeps their meat tender.

The United States Animal Welfare Act of 1966 (and its revision in 1970) provides that all animals should have a minimum space in which to stretch and turn around. This is called "freedom of movement," and it applies to all animals in zoos, pet stores, and research laboratories. However, animals

raised for food are an exception—this rule does not apply to them.

Thus there is a double standard when it comes to animal conditions and comfort. People are prosecuted for housing dogs and cats the way pigs are housed. This is curious when you consider that pigs have high intelligence—as much or more than dogs—and make trainable pets. A new pet fad, incidentally, is Vietnamese pot belly pigs.

Because meat eating is considered natural and enjoyable by millions of people, there is no reason to expect that people will stop eating animals any time soon. And while many animal rights activists may not be *vegetarians* (people who do not eat meat), they still believe that forcing livestock to live under inhumane circumstances is unnecessary for the raising of food.

What is needed to correct this situation is a change in the agricultural industry. Fewer animals should be raised in better conditions so that their lives are not filled with confinement, stress, and painful amputations. Of course this would raise the cost of livestock, and that means that everyone would have higher grocery bills. But perhaps for a meat-eating culture it is the least we can do to keep animals from suffering unnecessarily while they are alive.

The Fur Fury

In 1989 animal rights activists marched in 91 American cities on what has been called "Fur-Free Friday." This annual protest focuses on the killing of animals for wearing apparel. The marchers carried fur coats streaked with red paint and coffins filled with furs. "Fur is torture" and "Fur is murder" were typical slogans on the protest signs. Some marchers resorted to vandalism by breaking store windows where furs were sold.

Animal rights activists have been after the fur industry for a long time. They think it is wrong to wear the hide of an animal, especially when the animal died for no other reason. Furs are usually expensive, and the rarer the animal it comes from, the more expensive the fur. Furs can cost many thousands of dollars.

Once fur was necessary for humans to stay alive in cold climates, before humans learned to build adequate shelter, control fire, or make clothing from other materials. But furs have remained a popular cold-weather item well into this century. Some of the first Europeans to arrive in North America trapped and sold furs. It was an easy trade to start.

So began the hunting of millions of animals on this continent: otters, foxes, raccoons, bears, wolves, bison, and more. After shooting or trapping an ani-

Dog For Dinner?

Our diet is most often a result of the culture in which we grew up. For instance, most Americans love to drink milk and eat ice cream. Many Asians, however, find drinking animal milk revolting. Some cannot even digest it properly.

In many Asian countries, however, eating dog is quite acceptable. In 1990 two Cambodian immigrants in Long Beach, California, were prosecuted for killing a German shepherd—for dinner. A judge dismissed the case because it wasn't illegal, and the dog was killed humanely. The outcry this caused led the California state legislature to pass a law making it illegal to raise and kill dog for consumption. However, rabbits are still officially considered livestock in California, so this law does not apply to the family bunny.

As the attorney for the Cambodians said, "Why should somebody not be able to eat something just because it's cuddly?"

mal, the skinned carcass was often left to scavengers because the trapper only wanted the fur.

The "fight fur" movement believes that raising an animal in a cage, only to kill and skin it for its coat, is an outrage. Some fur fighters have gone to extremes to get their argument across. For example, people wearing furs have been splattered with paint and worse in public. This is assault, and it's illegal. Shops that carry fur have been broken into and even put out of business by these protesters. One person's work is another person's cruelty to animals.

In their haste to help animals on fur farms, some activists have stolen caged minks and released them into the wild. This is not as great an idea as it may sound, as many of these animals have been domesticated to the point where they can't survive in the wild on their own. If fur fighters want to save domesticated animals, they will have to make other plans to have them cared for.

And what about people who wouldn't wear a coat made from real fur, yet have leather items in their own wardrobe? Leather is made from an animal hide that has been plucked of hair and *tanned* (a drying process). Chances are you own a pair of shoes, or a purse or wallet, made from leather.

The Dilemma

If we are concerned about the rights of animals, then sooner or later we must face their ultimate right: to not be eaten. What is wrong with eating other animals? Most of us do. It is what we do from the time we're very young. The human digestive tract is perfectly suited for absorbing nutrients

A stockyard in Kansas City, Missouri, where cattle await their
last stop: the slaughterhouse.

from both animal and vegetable foods. Every
human being is living proof that eating the flesh of
others—plant or animal—is how we survive.

Some people don't eat animal flesh in any
form. Vegetarians eat only non-meat foods such as
fruits, grains, nuts, and vegetables. Some people
avoid red meat because they believe it is healthier.
It is true that our health is affected greatly by what
we eat. Much of the beef we eat is exposed to artifi-
cial substances like antibiotics, which are given to
the cattle while they're still alive. If enough of these
chemicals stay in the animal, it is transferred to the
meat we eat and into our bodies. Some researchers
believe these chemicals cause cancer. Some people
feel healthier as vegetarians, while others may not.

So the choice to eat or not eat meat for health reasons is still a matter of personal preference.

Other humans become vegetarians because they feel it is morally wrong to eat other animals. This is also a matter of personal choice. Just because humans can eat animals, and always have, does that mean we should keep eating animals? Humans eat meat because it is natural—and reinforced by our culture—so why should we change our diet to save a chicken that is going to be someone else's dinner anyway?

If you're a typical student, you probably like eating meat. Going with your friends to McDonald's for a burger or to Kentucky Fried Chicken after school is fun, and you like the taste of the food. It is pleasurable. You really don't stop to think about it, but that cheeseburger was a living thing at one time. Do you want to give that up?

When our concern doesn't always match our behavior, its called a dilemma. Humans confront many of these dilemmas every day. For example, we may like animals, but when we build houses they destroy the natural homes of rabbits and gophers. We believe in good health for everyone, but when we drive to work to earn money our cars pollute the air, which is unhealthy to breathe (and costs money to clean up). Most of us find it impossible to live a pure life in today's world, so we learn to compromise.

FIVE

EXTINCTION AND CAPTIVITY

Animal rights groups tend to pay the most attention to treatment of animals who are most visible such as cute and cuddly animals in overcrowded shelters, animals kept for medical research, and livestock raised for food. But the ongoing destruction of our environment contributes to the greatest loss of animals in the world. With air pollution, heavy farming and forestry, and water pollution, humans are killing off more species in less time than ever before. Extinction may be a natural process, but humankind is rushing this process as never before.

Destroying Habitats

The U.S. Endangered Species Act (ESA) of 1973 was passed to protect this country's wildlife. It states that certain areas of our country, whether privately or publicly owned, can be protected if it were the habitat of a species threatened with extinction. For instance, a new skyscraper could be prevented from being built if it was found that it would forever ruin the home of an endangered species.

The ESA has been used to save a number of species, even at the expense of a local economy. Whole industrial projects have been prevented because a new plant or construction site was in danger of destroying a single species. Where there might have been new factory jobs, there remains a bit of protected land.

Once a dam was not built because it would

have ruined the habitat of the snail darter, a small fish. In 1990, construction of a new astronomical observatory in Arizona was delayed because the proposed site was the only home of the Mt. Graham red squirrel.

In the Pacific Northwest, the northern spotted owl has been threatened by heavy timber cutting. Since the lumber industry is so important to that region, restricting tree cutting for lumber could result in economic hardship for local residents. When jobs are at stake, the protection of a lone species usually becomes a political issue. People start asking, "what's more important, owls or people?" Animal rights activists believe it's possible to serve both, but sometimes protecting a habitat will cause problems for humans.

Your own home or apartment was probably built on land that once fed hundreds of rabbits, squirrels, and the birds that preyed on them. Every change in the environment can harm another species. Does that mean we should stop building, or stop breathing? Obviously this is not possible. But there are things humans can do to lessen the damage they do to a species' environment. One way is through controlled, planned growth that combines the needs of humans with the existing sanctuary of a species. The two can coexist.

With every acre of natural habitat that humans destroy, more creatures are gone forever. Death is a natural part of life, but forced, hurried death brought on by poor use of our earth's resources is not natural. The cost of what

This sea lion's pup was born at the Bronx Zoo, a rare event for this mammal. Animals who are endangered in the wild are being helped by zoo programs which try to raise animals in captivity.

humans have done to the earth thus far has yet to be calculated.

As one anthropologist wrote, "The general public is greatly concerned about the slaughter of cute baby seals or giant pandas, but not as worried about the welfare of frogs and bats which...serve more vital functions in the world ecosystem."

Zoos

The zoo is a favorite place to take a family. We all love to see wild and exotic animals from faraway places, and go into the petting area to see and touch the baby animals. For millions of youngsters who will never see a farm, it's a chance to get acquainted with some fascinating creatures. Every species has exciting things to teach us.

Zoos have evolved in the past two decades into "animal parks." Many of these new facilities treat their animals with care and respect. Instead of cages with bars, animals are kept in large areas that resemble their own natural habitat as much as possible. Some zoos have tram rides that keep noisy and inconsiderate people at a greater distance from the animals than in old-style zoos.

Yet it is still captivity. The animals are not free to roam anywhere they want. Of course many animals in zoos today could not survive in the wild. Many are born in captivity, and their parents are unable to teach them how to survive on their own. Some instincts need to be reinforced by actual experience in the wild.

On the other hand, some species have been saved from extinction by being captured and taken to zoos, then allowed to breed under human control. The California condor, for example, may one day be saved in this way. This concern for saving rare species, even if it means they must live in captivity indefinitely, is generally seen as a positive thing for our fellow creatures.

Performing Animals

Animals are used a lot to entertain us. Seals, lions, chimpanzees, and parrots are all used in "wild animal" shows worldwide. These animals probably live in clean conditions and are fed well. Few people object to these activities. But do all animal performers enjoy easy and healthy lives?

Let's look at one popular form of animal entertainment: horse racing. Thousands of people go to racing tracks daily to watch horses race at top speed. Thoroughbreds, the type of horses used in long races, are beautiful animals. They have been bred especially for their speed and stamina. Today's thoroughbreds are literally born to race. And there is no denying their beauty.

Today the racing game is big business. Horse racing is a gambling sport, and always has been. With the increase in profits has come increasing demands for champion horses. Owners of horses seek every edge they can, like the best trainers and jockeys. Horses receive excellent care and food. They also receive drugs.

More and more horses on America's racetracks are being given steroids—the same type of drug some athletes use to increase their muscle fiber and stamina. Steroids do the same thing for horses, but not necessarily for the horse's benefit. Drugs can harm the horse, but as long as the drugs are suspected of giving it a chance to win, the owner of a horse may prefer to ignore the ill effects. Unfortunately, a horse can't just say no.

Some drugs given to race horses are used to prevent health problems like internal bleeding and swelling of the joints. But these are problems caused by racing itself. If the horse didn't race, it probably wouldn't need drugs to stay healthy in the first place. Other drugs are forbidden on racetracks because they may give the horse an "illegal" advantage that is considered cheating—they supposedly

Thoroughbred horses are bred to run, but the pace of racing often forces stables to use drugs to keep their stock healthy.

change the outcome of the race. But when thousands of dollars are at stake, many people don't care what the horse is on, as long as it wins.

Thoroughbreds are exposed to more than just drugs. They may run so hard that they literally die in mid-race of heart failure. Some collide with each other, or stumble on a bad track. The result is usually a shattered leg which cannot be repaired. Even if it were repairable, the horse would never be able to race again. And since the horse is only good for racing, it is usually "destroyed"—a racetrack term for putting the animal to death.

Purebred Pets

Another kind of performer is the purebred pet. Dogs and cats of breeding are placed into competitions by their owners. The animals are then judged on the characteristics of their breed: body form, coat, eye color, obedience, and more. This is seemingly harmless fun. Owners take pride in having an animal that is a perfect specimen of its breed.

Unfortunately, some of the traits that have been inbred by dog and cat breeders are actually harmful to the animal's health. Sight and hearing, hip, joint, and foot problems are just some of the complications that breeds can suffer when they get older. Some pets go to the veterinarian because of illness or accidents. But purebreds with severe features have to go just to have their special problems corrected. These problems would be completely avoidable if the animal had not been bred according to a human concept of good breeding.

Recently, the "puppy mill" industry has been

attacked by animal rights groups because filthy crowded conditions have been found on many puppy breeding farms in the United States. In May 1990, some California state legislators and the Humane Society of the United States announced a boycott of pet store dogs bred in six states: Kansas, Oklahoma, Arkansas, Missouri, Iowa, and Nebraska. The reason? These farms treated the breeding dogs like slaves.

Malnutrition, disease, inadequate shelter—all have been found on American breeding farms. The "stock" are female dogs who live their lives in small cages, being bred every time they are in heat (twice a year). After five years or so, when their litter size drops, they are usually killed.

The USDA is responsible for regulating puppy farms to make sure they comply with the Animal Welfare Act. Enforcement is difficult, however, because the federal government has less money every year to fund this program. The budget cutting and deficits of the 1980s have forced all agencies to trim their staffs. Meanwhile, pets continue to be a product, bought and sold like any other "thing."

SIX

SHARING THE PLANET

About one-half of the world's species live in tropical rain forests, from Latin America and Southeast Asia to the Pacific Islands and West Africa. Yet it is estimated that one acre of rain forest disappears every two seconds due to harvesting, construction and disease. In just one acre there are hundreds of thousands of animals and birds, and millions of insects. This means that if we lose thousands of acres of forest every hour, then millions of animals (and sometimes entire species) are lost every hour, every day, every year.

In the world's oceans, oil spills, sewage and other pollutants poison living coral reefs. In the United States alone, we have lost 54 percent of our wetlands—marshes and groves that are the breeding grounds of many species of birds and fish. Poaching has threatened elephants, sea turtles, rhinoceros, monkeys, giant cats, and other creatures all over the world. So why should we care about the disappearance of so many animals and species?

First, we don't know what harm we're doing to surviving animals every time another species dies off. For example, if an animal species is dependent upon an extinct one for food, then a chain reaction is set off: one species starves because the other was driven to extinction. It's impossible to know how the problem will be compounded by this species' death.

Second, every species lost is one less from which we can study and learn—still the best method we have for learning more about our world and ourselves. With fewer species existing every day, there are fewer clues to the mystery of life on earth and our part in it.

The third reason is the most emotional and therefore the one on which humans most often disagree. It is the moral question we have wrestled with in this book: Do animals have rights because they live and breath and reproduce and eat and run just like humans? Does their very existence give them the same rights as human beings to live free?

Animals that live on earth today do so because they have adapted to the conditions of their environment. They survive. If their adaptation to this planet is as natural as it was for human beings, then don't they deserve the same chance at living as we do? They may not build bridges or cure influenza, but they exist. Why should human beings have an automatic right to control their lives? If only, like Dr. Dolittle, we could talk to the animals.

In 1865, the United States finally brought all citizens under the protection of the Constitution with the end of slavery. In 1920, women finally won the right to vote. In 1971, people between age 18 and 21 were also given the right to vote. Perhaps in the next decade, an amendment will be added that will extend certain legal rights to animals. What would those rights be? Are certain minimum conditions for animal life necessary, and can they be imposed in all areas where humans are in control?

The late U.S. Supreme Court Justice William O. Douglas wrote once that one day "all of the forms of life...will stand before the court—the pileated woodpecker as well as the coyote and bear."

In a way, the animal rights debate is really a

debate about human rights as well. After all, if we can't agree on how to treat our fellow human beings, it's no wonder some people treat animals even worse. It's easy to mistreat living things when we call them inferior or different. Perhaps if we learn to treat other species on this planet with more respect and concern, we will treat our fellow human beings better as well.

For More Information

There are many organizations that can give you more information about their views on animal rights. Here are some names and addresses. You can always find others in your local public library.

The American Society for the Prevention of Cruelty to
	Animals (ASPCA)
441 E. 92nd St.
New York, NY 10128

The Animal Legal Defense Fund
1363 Lincoln Ave.
San Rafael, CA 94901

Association of Veterinarians for Animal Rights
15 Dutch St., Suite 500-A
New York, NY 10038-3779

The Fund for Animals
200 W. 57th St.
New York, NY 10019

The Humane Society of the United States (HSUS)
2100 L Street, NW
Washington, D.C. 20037

People for the Ethical Treatment of Animals (PETA)
P.O. Box 42516
Washington, D.C. 20008

Glossary

ACTIVIST. A person who participates in a social cause or movement to demand change. For example, animal rights activists want humans to treat other species with more respect.

BEHAVIORAL TESTING. The use of animals such as rodents or primates in controlled experiments. Psychologists use these tests to predict human reactions to similar events outside the laboratory.

CADAVER. A dead human body used for medical research.

DILEMMA. A problem with two equally unpleasant solutions.

DOMESTICATION. The taming and raising of animals for their meat and other by-products.

DRAIZE TEST. The laboratory procedure using animals to test irritating eye and skin effects.

HABITAT. The natural home or locality of an animal.

LD-50. The "lethal dose" test used in laboratories to determine the *toxicity* of a substance. The toxicity level is found when half (50 percent) of the test animals die after being exposed to, fed or injected with the substance.

LIVESTOCK. Domesticated animals bred for use on farms or for sale.

MORATORIUM. An open-ended ban on the hunting or fishing of a species.

OMNIVOROUS. Able to eat and digest both animals and plants.

POACHING. The illegal hunting of animals.

SPECIESISM. The belief that human beings are superior to all other forms of life on earth.

VEGETARIAN. A person who does not eat any meat.

VIVISECTION. The surgical examination of a live animal to study its organs and parts.

Bibliography

Books

Bright, Michael. *Killing for Luxury*. New York: Gloucester Press, 1988.

Matthiessen, Peter. *Wildlife in America* (Revised ed.). New York: Viking, 1987.

Singer, Peter. *Animal Liberation*, 2nd ed. New York: The New York Review of Books, 1990.

The World Almanac and Book of Facts 1991. Pharos Books: New York, 1990.

Periodicals

Biermann, Karl. "Why Animal Experimentation Should Continue." *The Humanist*, July/August 1990: 8-9, 50.

Cole, John R. "Animal Rights and Wrongs." *The Humanist*, July/August 1990: 12-14, 42.

Collard III, Sneed B. "Refocusing Animal Rights." *The Humanist*, July/August 1990: 10-11, 49.

Crist, Steven. "Racing Faces New Drug Problem." *The New York Times*, July 15, 1990: 16.

Elshtain, Jean Bethke. "Why Worry About the Animals?" *The Progressive*, March 1990: 17-23.

Goldberg, Alan M. and John M. Frazier. "Alternatives to Animals in Toxicity Testing." *Scientific American*, August 1989: 24-30.

Greene, Katherine and Richard. "Medical Research

Saved My Son's Life." *Redbook*, September 1989: 160.

HSUS News. The Humane Society of the United States. Fall, 1990, Vol. 35, No. 4.

LaGanga, Maria L. "Thousands Demonstrate Against Sales of Furs." *The Los Angeles Times*, November 25, 1989: D2.

Marcus, Erin. "New Research Methods Seen Unlikely to Eliminate Animal Testing." *The Washington Post*, August 28, 1990: A3.

Mouras, Belton P. "Lifting the Curtain on Animal Labs." *USA Today*, March 1988: 48-51.

Sleeper, Barbara. "The Puppy Mill Connection." *Animals*, November/December 1990: 10-13.

Trull, Frankie L. "Animal Research." *USA Today*, March 1988: 52-54.

Zak, Steven. "Ethics and Animals." *The Atlantic Monthly*, March 1989: 69-74.

About The Author

Gregory Lee has edited more than 100 books for juveniles and adults, including books on American society and government, geopolitics and even martial arts. A journalism graduate from California State University, Northridge, Greg is now a freelance writer and book packager. He lives in Laguna Hills, California, with his wife and three cats.

INDEX

Picture Credits

All photographs by AP/Wide World

Riverside
County

LIBRARY SYSTEM

www.rivlib.net